HOMER'S ILIAD

Ancient Greece Books for Teens
Children's Ancient History

BABY PROFESSOR

EDUCATION KIDS

Speedy Publishing LLC

40 E. Main St. #1156

Newark, DE 19711

www.speedypublishing.com

Copyright 2017

In this book, we're going to talk about the famous poem of Greek Literature called The Iliad. So, let's get right to it!

LYRE

WHAT IS AN EPIC POEM?

In Ancient times, long, narrative stories were often told by singing to the accompaniment of a lyre, which is a musical instrument that looks like a small U-shaped harp. For centuries, these stories weren't written down, so the singers and poets who presented them had to know them by heart. Eventually, these stories were retold many times and poets wrote them down by putting the best of the oral traditions down on paper.

Sometime between 725 and 675 BC, the Greek poet by the name of Homer wrote down the story we now know as The Iliad, an epic poem. It is not known whether Homer actually created the story or whether he took down the ideas of the oral traditions and rewrote it into the form we can read today. Historians also don't know for sure whether The Iliad and The Odyssey were written exclusively by him or whether a group of authors worked on them.

HOMER

HOMER

In the original Greek language the poem doesn't rhyme, but it is written in a specific meter called dactylic hexameter, a type of quantitative meter that is very difficult to write in English. Translators who worked with the ancient poem to translate it into English and other languages rewrote it in rhyming heroic couplets. The Iliad has over 15,000 lines and takes about eight hours to read, so it's hard to believe that minstrel poets and singers could perform it by heart, but they did and the poem has some repetitive structure just like a song that has a chorus. Homer fills the poem with similes and metaphors so that images and feelings within the poem remain memorable.

WHAT IS THE ILIAD ABOUT?

The war between the Trojans and the Greeks lasted for ten years. The narrative of The Iliad takes place over several months during the war's tenth year. The history of the Trojan War would have been discussed and sung about frequently in Ancient times. Homer's audiences and readers would have understood when he made reference to events that had happened before the time period of The Iliad.

TROJAN WAR

ΙΟ ΤΟΝ ΑСΠΑΙΠ ΓΟΛΟΦΥΡΑΤΟ ΛΑΚΗ ΥΧΕΟΝΙΑ
ΥСΣΕΛΘΟ ΙΛΛΟΝ СΟΟΝ ΕΜ ΜΕΝΑΙΟΥΛ ΠΟΛΕ СΟΛΙ
ΙΚ ΑΛΛΙСΤΟΝΙΙΚΕΓΕΛ СΙΟΤΑΓΟΝ ΠΕ ΤΗΝ СΩΝ
ΟΝ ΕΧΟΝ ΤΟΝ ΥΧ ССΙΤ ΕΚΟ СΕΛ ΑΦΟΙΟ ΤΑΧΕΙΙ С
ΑΙΟ СΒ ΒΩΔ ΙСΩ Ι ΠΕ ΓΙΚΑ ΛΛ ΑΓΙ ΚΑ ΒΒΑ ΛΕΝ ΕΒΙΓΟΝ
ΤΑΝΟ Ι ΦΛΙ СΩΙΖΗ ΝΙ ΓΕ ΖΕ С ΚΟΝ ΑΧ ΛΙΟΙ
СΟΥΝ ΙΔ ΟΝΟ ΟΓΑΓΕΚ ΑΙΟСΙ ΛΥΟΕΝΟΓΝΙС
ΛΟΝ СΙ ΠΡ СωΕ ССΙΟ ΟΤ ΟΝ ΥΗ ΙΙС ΑΝΤΟ ΛΕΧΑΡΙΤΙ
СΟΥ ΠΕ ΠΙС ΓΟ ΡΟ ΛΛΙ ΑΔ ΝΙΥ ΟΛ ΛΕΧ ΙΙ СΩΝΤΙ

MAIN CHARACTERS OF THE ILIAD

There are many characters in The Iliad and it helps to become familiar with them before reading the poem.

ON THE GREEK SIDE OF THE BATTLE

ACHILLES

Achilles is the central character in the story. He is the most successful warrior in the world at that time. He is the leader of a Greek tribe called the Myrmidons.

ACHILLES

AGAMEMNON

Agamemnon is the Greek army general. Although both he and Achilles are fighting on the Greek side against the Trojans, they are always arguing and don't get along. There is a power struggle between them.

MENELAUS

Menelaus is the king of the Greek city-state of Sparta. His wife Helen, who is thought to be the woman possessing the most beauty in the whole world, has been kidnapped by a Trojan man by the name of Paris. This is the initial reason that the Greeks and Trojans are at war with each other.

HELEN

Even goddesses are jealous of Helen due to her great beauty. She is the wife of Menelaus, but after the goddess of love Aphrodite puts a spell on her she falls in love with Paris and he kidnaps her. She is "the face that launched a thousand ships" as the Greeks sail to bring her back from Troy.

HELEN OF TROY

ODYSSEUS

Odysseus is a famous warrior hero who is also known for his great intellectual capacity.

AIAS THE GREAT

Aias is another great warrior of the Greek army, second only to Achilles.

ON THE TROJAN SIDE OF THE BATTLE

PRIAM

Priam is the Trojan king during the time period that The Iliad takes place.

HECUBA

Hecuba is the Trojan queen. Priam and Hecuba have nineteen children together including their son Hector.

HECUBA

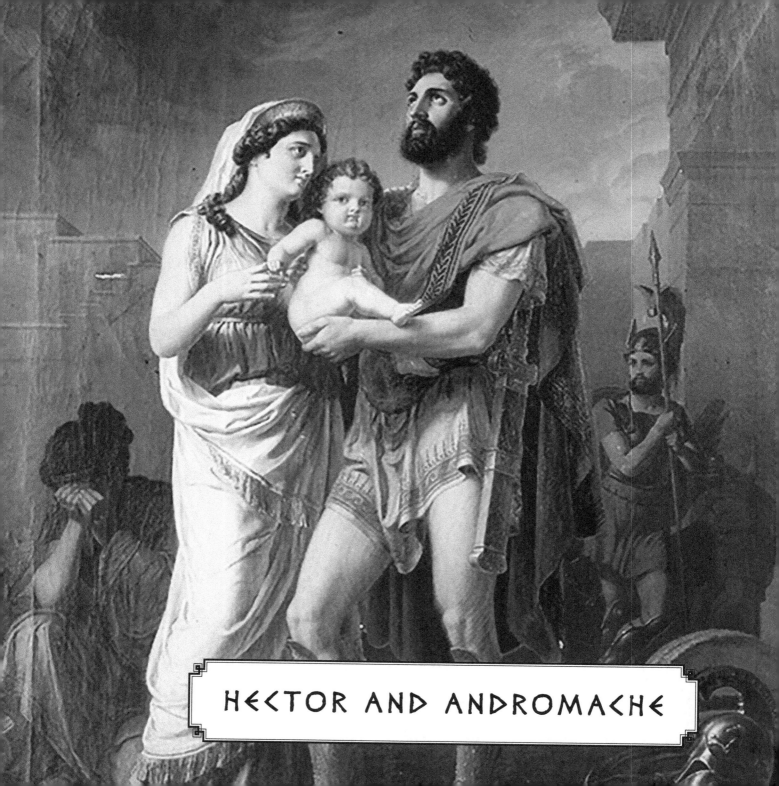

HECTOR AND ANDROMACHE

HECTOR

The oldest son of Priam and Hecuba, Hector is the most masterful of all the Trojan warriors.

ANDROMACHE

Andromache is the wife of Hector.

PARIS

Paris was long in love with the beautiful wife of King Menelaus, named Helen. When Paris was asked to judge a beauty contest of three goddesses, he proclaims Aphrodite the winner since she bribes him by arranging for Helen to be his. This kidnapping of Helen by Paris is what starts the 10-year Trojan War.

AENEAS

Aeneas is the second most powerful Trojan warrior after Hector.

AENEAS FLEEING FROM TROY

Several gods and goddesses of Greek mythology take sides in the Battle as well. Zeus who is the king of all the gods

and goddesses tries to remain neutral but is eventually persuaded to help the Trojans.

SUMMARY OF THE PLOT

The Greeks have set up camp outside the walls of the citadel of Troy. Achilles is arguing with Agamemnon over a woman slave.

THE TROJAN HORSE BROUGHT
INTO THE CITADEL OF TROY

ACHILLES' SLAVE, BRISEIS,
HANDED OVER TO AGAMEMNON

This slave was given to Achilles because of his masterful fighting. When Agamemnon takes this woman away from Achilles, he goes into a fury and then eventually loses his desire to continue to fight.

During this time, Hector, who is the son of the Trojan King, attacks the Greeks and drives them into the sea. When Hector kills Patroclus, who was a close friend to Achilles, this prompts Achilles to action again. The Greeks are able to push the Trojans back behind the walls of their citadel once more.

THE RAGE OF ACHILLES

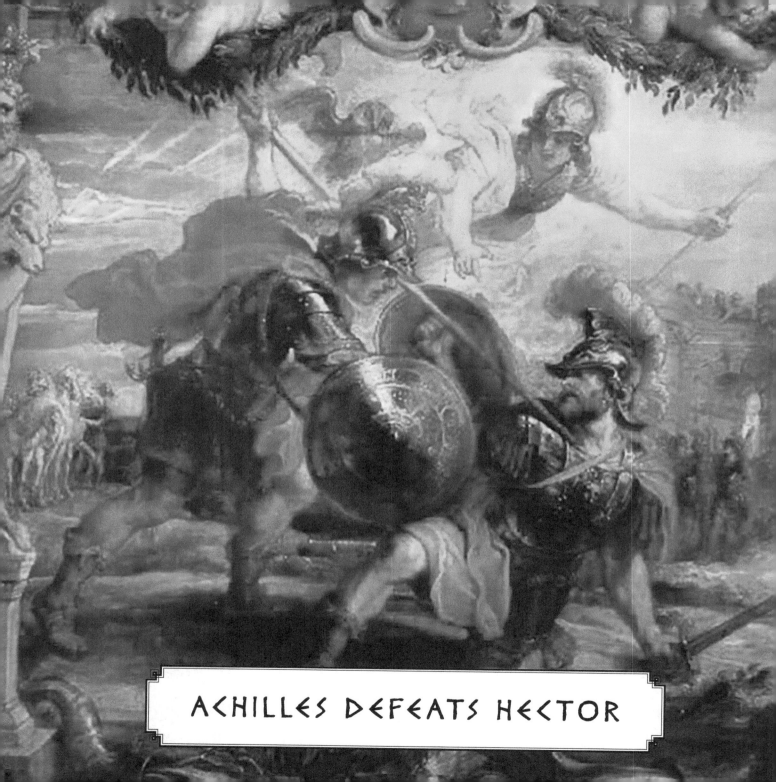

ACHILLES DEFEATS HECTOR

During the ensuing battles, Achilles defeats Hector and he dies. Achilles takes his anger out on Hector's dead body, but eventually returns the corpse to Hector's father so that he can have a hero's burial.

The poem concludes before some other decisive events of the Trojan War including the arrow that strikes Achilles's heel and kills him and the story of the Greeks and how they enter behind the walls of Troy inside a huge wooden horse.

1c

ACHILLES DYING

TROJAN FORTRESS

WHEN THE STORY OPENS

The battle between Troy and Greece has been going on for a decade and yet the Greeks seem no closer to infiltrating the Trojan fortress.

THE ARGUMENT BETWEEN ACHILLES AND AGAMEMNON

Greek soldiers are dying of a mysterious plague. A soothsayer, a person who can see the future, says that the plague has happened because Agamemnon has not returned a woman named Chryseis who had been awarded to him after a battle with Troy.

THE AMBASSADORS OF AGAMEMNON
VISITING ACHILLES

QUARREL BETWEEN ACHILLES
AND AGAMEMNON

Her father had pleaded with Agamemnon to release her and he even offered money to the great general, but Agamemnon refused. But, when her father prays to Apollo, the sun god begins attacking Agamemnon's army. Achilles and others force him to release Chryseis, but to get revenge on Achilles, Agamemnon takes the woman named Briseis who had been given to Achilles.

ACHILLES LOSES MOTIVATION

Achilles becomes so angry that he stops fighting for the Greeks. He asks his mother, the goddess Thetis, if she will plead his case to Zeus the king of the gods. Achilles asks that Zeus help the Trojans who were Achilles's enemies. Zeus has remained neutral until now, but he starts helping the Trojans at the request of Thetis.

THETIS AND ZEUS

Thetis has always been fearful that her son Achilles will die young. As an infant, she held him in the River Styx so that the magical waters would strengthen him, but because she was holding him by the heel it was never protected like the rest of this body. His heel is the weakest part of this body. This is where the expression "Achilles' Heel" comes from.

THE FIGHT GOES FORWARD

Both sides are weary of the conflict, but the battle continues as the gods become more entangled. When Hector is felled by a giant stone that was thrown by the Greek warrior Aias, the sun god Apollo heals Hector's wounds and makes him even more powerful than he was previously. Hector's new power helps the Trojan army attack. The Greek army retreats to the shore.

APOLLO

DEATH OF PATROCLUS

PATROCLUS DIES

It looks inevitable that the Greeks will lose the war. Patroclus, Achilles's friend, goes to him to beg him to come back into the fight, but Achilles won't budge. Patroclus puts on his friend's armor and goes into the battle. The Greeks are gaining until Hector confronts Patroclus, kills him, and takes Achilles's armor.

ACHILLES COMES BACK TO THE BATTLE

Now Achilles is angrier than ever. He must avenge the death of his best friend. The god of the forge, Hephaestus, creates a new armor for Achilles and he and his Greek forces go on the attack and push the Trojans back inside their city. Achilles meets Hector on the battlefield and they fight for a long time until Achilles defeats Hector and he dies. This is where The Iliad ends, but there is more to the story.

THETIS RECEIVING THE WEAPONS OF ACHILLES FROM HEPHAESTUS

DEATH OF ACHILLES

ACHILLES DIES

The sun god Apollo is still helping the Trojans in their battles. When Paris shoots an arrow toward Achilles, Apollo guides the arrow to strike Achilles in his weak and vulnerable heel. Achilles dies quickly after the poisoned arrow strikes him.

THE TROJAN HORSE

ventually, the Greeks come up with a grand scheme to defeat the Trojans. They hide inside a large wooden horse and the Trojans pull them inside the city's gates. Once inside they come out of their hiding place and are able to take the Trojans by surprise and with the war.

Awesome! Now you know more about the Homer's epic poem, The Iliad. You can find more Ancient History books from Baby Professor by searching the website of your favorite book retailer.

Visit

BABY PROFESSOR
EDUCATION KIDS

www.BabyProfessorBooks.com

to download Free Baby Professor eBooks and view
our catalog of new and exciting Children's Books

CPSIA information can be obtained
at www.ICGtesting.com
Printed in the USA
BVHW062053010319
541617BV00002B/13/P

9 781541 911222